# Friendship and Love

## JANET LUMB

**Scripture Union**
130 City Road, London EC1V 2NJ

© 1988 Janet Lumb

First published 1988
Reprinted 1990

Lumb, Janet
  Friendship and love.
  1. Christian life. Friendship
  I. Title
  248.4

ISBN 0–86201–525–1

Phototypeset by Input Typesetting Ltd., London.
Printed and bound in Great Britain by
Cox & Wyman Ltd., Reading

# Contents

## Thanks . . .

to all the young friends who
have helped me write this –
whether they know it or not.

# 1
# From friendship to love

Quite a few books have been written for people with big problems in their relationships. This isn't one of them. And it's not written for those who are thinking of getting married soon. A lot of the issues they will need to consider are different. This book has been written for people who want to make good relationships, particularly with the opposite sex.

There are many voices telling you how to think and act. The one voice that you need to hear is God's. How far *do* you go? *Is* it wrong to go out with a non-Christian? Is something wrong with you if you *don't* have a boyfriend/girlfriend? What has the Bible got to say, if anything, on these things?

Don't bother reading any further unless you want to find out what God wants. It would be wasting your time. But if you do, fasten your seat belt! You might get a rough ride, but you will find there certainly *are* answers – not always easy, but always the best. God who made you knows how best to run your life.

Did you know that 'going out' is a modern invention, and that it is the custom in some countries, but not in others?

Perhaps the word 'invention' surprises you. We are led to understand that 'going out' is a part of nature and not a habit that people have thought of for themselves. But it is something modern. In Cameroon, Christians think that kissing should wait for engagement at least!

A friend of mine, whose family is from Pakistan, was very alarmed because her father brought a young guy over to England, intending her to marry him. She found that too much to ask, because she was used to the British way of doing things.

In 'Olde Englande', marrying off your son or daughter so that you could gain money or power, was common. Love might grow out of marriage, if you were lucky, but was not allowed to grow into it. (Think about it!) Arranged marriages are still common in some countries today but the whole process is often much more thoughtful. Parents try to consider what the young people want, and what would be best for them. Free choice in love has been accepted in this country for more than 100 years – you breathe a sigh of relief!

The Bible has plenty to say about friendship, and a lot to say about marriage. But, as you may have noticed, nothing about 'going out'. So we're going to have to dig deep to find out what God has to say on the subject. He does, in fact, have a lot to say. To really hear what he says, we have to find out how the principles in the Bible relate to our lives in the kind of world we live in today.

# Talking point

Why do you think 'going out' was invented?

# 2
## Friendship - the key

Who do you talk to if you're in trouble? Probably your friend.

David was in some amazing messes. His life was in danger. He had to run away. He turned to his friend Jonathan. They had an exceptionally close friendship. They were 'one in spirit' (but not 'one in flesh' as in marriage). They had to arrange to meet secretly, because Jonathan's father Saul was out to get David. Jonathan was willing to do anything to help David. They cried together, shared their deepest troubles, and made a special promise of commitment to each other. Read 1 Samuel 18 onwards, for the whole story.

I'd like to suggest that friendship is the key to all good relationships. If you want a boyfriend or girlfriend, first get yourself a boy friend or girl friend, or rather, several. Learn how girls tick – or boys. One of the friendships might develop and become special. If it doesn't, you are not left hanging about, because you have a good circle of friends, you enjoy their company, you can talk to them.

But that might be difficult, you are thinking? Imagine the following scene: Boy meets girl at party. They are attracted to each other, by how they look, by witty jokes, by mannerisms. They get talking. They get kissing. They are 'going out'. You know that's about normal in the way things develop. There are a whole lot of questions surrounding that. But the main one is this. Do the boy and girl know one another well enough to start 'going out'? What have they based their relationship on? In their case, the attraction comes first. The friendship either comes afterwards or it doesn't. In which case they 'break up'. That means they stop 'going out' together, and perhaps avoid each other, or don't speak to each other. If they do become good friends, that's great. The friendship is quite likely to be weak though, because it wasn't built on much to begin with. If you start with friendship, it develops much more naturally. You find out what you have in common, how you see things, what you like and hate, what you would die for . . . If you find you share the same interests, and think the same way about a lot of things, you get to know each other better and see each other more often. Then you are 'going out'. And you know what you are letting yourself in for. Your life is also rich because you have other friends, not just the one. You have spent time getting to know a variety of people. You have had the time to find out what sort of a boy or girl you really like.

Because 'going out' is the custom, a lot of people are forced into it too soon. They are afraid there is something wrong with them if they aren't 'going out' with someone, so they go out with almost anyone, rather than no one! They watch what people around them are doing, and do the same.

It will come as no surprise to you that, as Christians are to be different in every area of life, they are to be different in this one. Not just different for the sake of it but different because God's way of doing things is actually better and will make us happier. Although 'going out' relationships between friendship and marriage are common in this country, it is just as possible to have

FRIENDSHIP▶MARRIAGE

as: FRIENDSHIP▶GOING OUT▶MARRIAGE

or: GOING OUT▶MARRIAGE.

We'll think more later about how that can work.

The point I am making in this chapter is that if you have a good friendship you have something good in itself. It is a foundation you might or might not build on later to make a closer relationship. It is a foundation which will stay firm, even if your friend should become ill or unattractive, or be tired. It is actually what you need to make any good relationships. So work on making good friends of both sexes.

You may find that people think you are strange to do this, even bent. Some boys in particular avoid making friends of the same sex for fear of what people might think! Carol says that in her area some people are more suspicious of a girl who shares a house with another girl than of one who shares with a guy! Being a Christian often means resisting pressures like this from people who love to look for problems. Jesus had friends who were women. Remember the woman who poured expensive perfume on his feet? She had a bad reputation for her past behaviour with men, so you can imagine what people were saying behind Jesus' back.

If they had looked at his pure life they would have known he could offer friendship to both sexes. His friendships had no 'hint of sexual immorality' (Ephesians 5:3). He had a special friendship with the disciple John and the Bible talks about him as 'the disciple whom Jesus loved'.

Listen to Paul's good advice to Timothy about how to treat others: 'Treat younger men as brothers, older women as mothers, and younger women as sisters, with absolute purity' (1 Timothy 5:1–2).

---

## Talking point

What is a good friendship? How do you make good friendships?

# 3
# Appearance is deceptive

When you look at yourself, do you see what others see? Probably not. You might see big ears, hair in a mess, a HUGE spot in the middle of your forehead. They probably see a smiling face, a cheerful and friendly manner. When we look at ourselves critically, we can sometimes magnify our faults because we have some sort of 'ideal' in our mind's eye of what we should be like. So the spot becomes a mountain, the ears wings, the hair a haystack.

When you size up potential girlfriends or boyfriends, are you comparing them, too, with the model you saw in a magazine recently? Do you think you would really like to go out with someone like that? Why?

Appearance is important, but it can give the wrong impression. You have probably read in the newspapers about girls who have fallen in love with a kind, gentle stranger, who turned out to be a conman. They were taken in by appearances (and conmen are very clever, probably most of us would be fooled). Have you ever thought someone was stuck up, only to find, once you got to know them, that they were simply shy? Or have you thought someone was miserable, and then you discovered it's just the way their mouth turns? You know what it has felt like when people have thought things about you which weren't true.

So should we ignore appearances and judge people by their character alone? Appearance generally does express *something*, so it is unwise to disregard it altogether. But it's important to learn just how much appearance *can* say, and so avoid misreading people by their looks.

If someone is kind, it shows in their warm face. If cruel, in hard eyes. It is difficult to hide a cheerful personality, it comes out at all the edges. If someone has lovely fair hair, God (or a bottle?) has given it to them. You might find it attractive – that's your view of beauty – but you haven't found out yet whether he or she is nice or nasty as a person.

The trouble is, we have been given so many pictures of what the ideal man or woman should be like that we can hardly help being attracted to someone who looks like the one in the advert or magazine, or wherever it is we look for our ideals. It becomes a problem when we are *obsessed* with appearance, our own or someone else's, because then we overlook more important things about a person.

What happens when we think too much about what *we* look like?

**1.** We are always aware of what we look like, and how other people might be thinking about us. We can't relax and be natural. We become so stiff that people wonder if we are real!

**2.** We take every little comment about our appearance personally, and are easily upset. We end up with very little confidence in ourselves, and look the worse for being miserable!

**3.** We spend too much time or money (depending on which we have more of) buying or thinking about clothes, hairstyles and make-up.

What happens when we think too much about what other people look like?

**1.** We miss out on a lot of lovely people who don't happen to have the physique or hair or face we have decided we like.

**2.** We forget to choose our friends on the basis of more important qualities.

**3.** We are likely to find it hard to relate to someone who does meet all the conditions of the 'ideal' person because the picture we have of him or her is more imaginary than real. When we meet him or her face to face, our knees go weak, our mouth dries up and we can only mumble a few disjointed words!

It is easy to make the mistake of weighing someone up on what they look like. When Samuel was looking for the person God wanted to be king, he thought he spotted the right one straight away. But God said, 'Do not consider his appearance or his height, for I have rejected him. The Lord does not look at the things man looks at. Man looks at the outward appearance, but the Lord looks at the heart' (1 Samuel 16:7).   If we can learn to see people more as God sees them we'll find beauty in unexpected places.

Have you read about the ideal wife, described in

Proverbs chapter 31? She has 'noble character'. She 'sets about her work vigorously; her arms are strong for her tasks' – a muscular pin-up?! The person who spotted her knew what to look for. He said: 'Charm is deceptive, and beauty is fleeting; but a woman who fears the Lord is to be praised' (Proverbs 31:30).

But in case you think God didn't notice how attractive he made the opposite sex, look at Solomon's song, where a man talks about the woman he loves, and is about to marry:

'Your eyes behind your veil are doves.
Your hair is like a flock of goats . . .
Your teeth are like a flock of sheep . . .
your lips are like a scarlet ribbon;
your mouth is lovely . . .'

. . . and so it goes on! (Song of Songs 4:1–3.) You might want to look for different ways of describing the features of the man you love! But certainly the couple are aware of each other's beauty. The woman describes the man too, as:

'. . . radiant and ruddy,
outstanding among ten thousand.
His head is purest gold;
his hair is wavy
and black as a raven.
His eyes are like doves . . .
His cheeks are like beds of spice . . .
His lips are like lilies . . .'

(Song of Songs 5:10-13). She says of her new husband:

'This is my lover, this is my friend.'

She has been knocked over by what he looks like – but not so that she forgot to get to know him properly as a friend. She is not so cold that she doesn't notice his attractiveness.

As you get to know people, you see what is really attractive in them. You notice things about them you *couldn't* see until you *knew* them. You respond to the personality that shows through in their face and actions. This beauty is more than skin deep.

---

## Talking point

To what extent should you be bothered about what you look like?

# 4
## Fantasy versus reality

Sandra had her own idea of a dream lover. This was fed mainly by the magazines she read, and her favourite star. It wasn't just a passing thought: she imagined meeting him, going out with him, being swept off her feet. There was no real likelihood she would meet him, of course. But, without realizing it, she compared all the boys she met with him. Blonde hair, brown eyes, high cheekbones, a gentle smile just for her. Whenever she met someone roughly like that, and with muscles in all the right places, she melted. She used all her powers to attract him. Sometimes she succeeded in holding his attention. Occasionally the conversation led to meeting up again and going out. The funny thing was, it never lasted. Either she was so frozen up she couldn't be herself, and he soon backed off, or she discovered he was rude, selfish or a bore. Funnier still, she didn't learn. She kept being attracted to people with similar characteristics and went on being disappointed by the reality behind them.

As well as having an ideal for her guy to live up to, Sandra had one for herself. But when she tried to live up to it, it never quite came off. She became bad-tempered instead of charming; stupid and stumbling instead of witty. She ended up dissatisfied both with herself and with her guys. They never quite came up to the image in her mind. Poor Sandra! Where did she go wrong?

Some people don't want to face reality! They would rather live in a world of fantasy. There the heroes and heroines are good-looking, brave and gentle. Nothing goes really wrong in their relationships or at least, if it does, there is always another one round the corner. There are plenty of magazines and songs to create that kind of picture.

Living in a fantasy world can be dangerous. You don't want to come out of it – life is too hard. If you bury yourself in imaginary relationships with imaginary people who are everything you want in every way, you will be disappointed with real people. They are not like that! The attractive thing about a dream world is that it's not so important for you to be perfect yourself. Not many demands are made on you. The other person is the busy one, making everything all right for you.

Some people do not develop real relationships very far, because they never live up to the ones they have imagined. This is very sad for them.

Even worse is an imagined relationship with a *real* person. Jesus spoke very strongly about people who have wrong sexual thoughts about someone they know: 'You have heard that it was said, "Do not commit adultery." But I tell you that anyone who looks at a woman lustfully has already committed adultery with her in his heart' (Matthew 5:27,28). Thoughts of this nature are so unfair on the other person. It makes them less than a person, more a plaything. Even so, it can be a strong temptation for some.

Having a fantasy world is a way of avoiding the pressures of real life. If you have a fantasy world, you can escape into it as often as you like. It is much easier than relating to people in the real world. That's why it is dangerous. By living in a fantasy world, you miss out on the opportunities which real relationships provide – opportunities to grow up and become a more complete person. Living in the real world also helps you to face and overcome real problems! That way, you become stronger.

Having a fantasy world may also mean you try to create something like it in real life. You look for someone who seems nearest to your dream boyfriend or girlfriend. You expect him or her to be all the things you have imagined. He/she isn't, of course, and you become disillusioned. He or she is a disappointment. The first attraction melts away. You either become bored, or dislike the person as strongly as you once liked him or her. You move on, trying someone else, still hoping the ideal boyfriend or girlfriend will turn up.

Your fantasy world and reality never meet. Maybe the person who seems most like your dream guy or girl turns out to be the least pleasant. You might know others who have a lot of qualities of character you like and admire but, because they lack the fantasy qualities, you won't bother to get to know them. So reality never satisfies. You have built a dream world which you won't give up. You either can't make good relationships at all, or you have one relationship after another, always looking for the ideal which doesn't exist.

The only way to avoid this trap is to spend more time with *real* people! Give the mags a miss, concentrate on getting to know people well. Come to terms with their faults – and your own. Learn to listen; learn to care. The people in a fantasy world have no faults, or only attractive ones. Real relationships involve pain, difficulty, struggle, as your faults and those of the other person meet. You negotiate, learn to adapt to each other, and knock off the rough edges: 'As iron sharpens iron, so one man sharpens another' (Proverbs 27:17).

Don't avoid this side of a relationship. Welcome it. It is the only way to a deep relationship. The relationship which has nothing to overcome is fairly superficial. The relationship which has come through a difficult problem, or a row or a hurt, is better for it. It shows its strength by what it can stand. A relationship which is knocked over by an argument was a flimsy thing.

In the end, reality is better than fantasy. There is only really you in the fantasy world, and it gets lonely. Real people, for all their faults, keep you company, talk to you, go about with you, make you laugh. They are made in God's image. Although it's distorted, they still reflect something of what God is like.

---

## Talking point

How can you come out of a fantasy world?

# 5
# *How do you see yourself?*

'He'd make a lovely husband, but I wouldn't want to go out with him.' Have you heard this kind of logic (or non-logic)? One of the things it could mean is that here is an extremely nice person, but he hasn't got the physical features/car/status that would make me want to be seen with him. Is it possible to go deeper, and find real beauty?

Have you, first of all, come to terms with what you are yourself? We've already noticed that it is possible to have the wrong impression of what we look like. The boy whose friends call him 'ears' thinks they are like an elephant's. The girl with a little extra weight here and there thinks she is too big to fit into a three-seater settee.

This twisted picture of yourself can go further. You drop a cup two weeks running, and think you are clumsy. You hear the sound of your own voice, and think you are a bore. Your joke falls like a lead balloon, and you never crack one again! Or perhaps you once played two notes right on the piano, and think you are heading for a musical career. Or a walk-on part in the school play has made you think you are destined for a life of theatrical stardom.

If any of us can take two steps back from ourselves, we have to laugh. What tangles we are!

But why am I talking about you, if we are meant to be thinking about how you relate to other people? Because what you think and feel about yourself has a very big effect on how you treat others. Have you heard of the 'little man' complex? A person who is small might feel he is looked down upon because of his size, so he bosses everyone else around, to prove he is not inferior. If he felt happy with the size he was, he wouldn't feel the need to prove himself. This kind of thing happens with all of us.

Try thinking about some part of your character you don't like. First of all, ask God if it's something you need to change, in other words, something you shouldn't be like. You may find the answer to this question becomes clear. If not, you may want to talk to someone else – an older person you trust or a friend who knows you well. But don't get bogged down. If you feel this part of you needs to change, ask God to help you. If not, thank him for it. Ask him to make use of it, whether it is your ability to lead, your quality of making friends with anybody and everybody or your knack of calming down a quarrel. Then accept yourself, complete with that and all the combination of characteristics that God has given you. But don't spend too long thinking about yourself. The picture will definitely get distorted if you do.

Think about these words from Psalm 139:

> 'For you created my inmost being;
>   you knit me together in my mother's womb.
> I praise you because I am
>   fearfully and wonderfully made' (verses 13,14).

Can you say that about yourself? It doesn't mean there are no peculiarities in you, or that everything is perfect about you. It does mean that God has created you *you*, with a unique combination of characteristics, gifts and qualities. Thank him for making you like that.

If you are at ease in your own skin, you can relax with others. You accept yourself; you accept that they'll be able to accept you. You have a certain amount of confidence. You don't need to prove anything to anyone. You can relax and smile!

Even more important than accepting yourself is knowing that God, the Lord of heaven and earth, accepts you – just as you are. He doesn't say, 'When you are all I want you to be, I'll let you into my kingdom.' Rather, he says in effect, 'Repent and come into my kingdom, and I will begin to make you what I want you to be.'

You might call for a friend. If you are told, 'Wait here, I'll get him,' and are left standing on the doorstep in the cold, you might feel very uncomfortable. If the person who answers the door says, 'Come in; sit down,' and draws you into the family circle for a laugh and a joke, you will probably feel much happier. Our Lord has drawn us in. We can 'sit down' and be one of the family.

It is good to be wanted; then we can start to make other people feel accepted and important.

## Talking point

Try telling yourself your good qualities. Or if you are in a group who all know each other well (not otherwise) try this, for five or ten minutes. Each draws a simple self-portrait, then passes it around the circle. As each one comes round, you write on it one of the good qualities of that person. (It will probably be necessary for each person to put their name on their picture, in case it isn't recognized!)

# 6
# *People matter*

I am important because God made me and loves me; other people are important for the same reason. Do you put a high value on other people?

'Look at the birds of the air; they do not sow or reap or store away in barns, and yet your heavenly Father feeds them. Are you not much more valuable than they?' (Matthew 6:26).

If you begin to appreciate God's love for other people, you will begin to love them too. If you see them with his eyes, you will begin to be interested in how they are, what is important to them, what would help them. You will be able to stop looking at yourself so much, worrying how *you* are and what *your* needs are.

As you are drawn out to think about other people, you become very attractive. People will look for your company and enjoy being with you. They will be glad to be counted your friend. But that is by the way. 'In everything, do to others as you would have them do to you' (Matthew 7:12). You know what you enjoy, what makes you feel good, what you long for people to say to you to encourage you. Try it out on others!

Other people are the same as you, and they are different from you.

They are the same as you in that if you say something harsh, if you criticize them, if you joke about their appearance, they will be hurt. If you say how good they are at something, if you praise their achievements whatever they are, if you admire their good points, they will be happy. It's as simple as that. Try the positive approach! Everyone is sensitive inside, not only you. Everyone is easily hurt, as well as you.

And people are different from you. Not everyone reacts in the same way. Not everyone likes the same things. Pete loves to have his girlfriend beside him at the football match. His girlfriend hates football. She loves it when Pete sits down with her and starts an interesting conversation. Mark likes nothing better than an evening at home watching telly. His friend Steve likes action; he wants to be out and among people.

So in learning to value people, you need to remember how you would like them to treat you. You also need to find out what their preferences are, and respect that.

Never see people as less important than you, 'but in humility consider others better than yourselves' (Philippians 2:3). Don't be tempted by the magazines, the television and videos, to treat other people as characters in a drama rather than as real people. Fictitious characters don't bleed (only stage blood), don't really hurt (they're only acting their tears) or get angry, or afraid. At the end of the story or film the characters are no more. But real people go home. They still exist. Like you, they think over the events of the day there. They cry if they have been hurt. They remember nice things people said about them, and store them up in their stock of pleasant memories.

How you treat people in all your relationships matters, not only the ones you like best or even only the ones you like at all. It is easiest, of course, to try to please those you hope will like you. Jesus said, 'If you love those who love you, what credit is that to you? Even "sinners" love those who love them. And if you do good to those who are good to you, what credit is that to you?' (Luke 6:32–33).

It is a good idea to practise understanding how the other person feels. It changes how you see them; it affects how you treat them. Is your friend bad-tempered? Why do you think that is? Has he or she got problems which are difficult to cope with? To think about the other person's needs is to begin to love as God loves.

## Talking point

How might you judge people wrongly? How can you show your friends they matter?

# 7
## Love me

Recently I saw a girl wearing a T-shirt with the words 'LOVE ME' written across it in large letters. That could mean different things to different people, but in a way we'd all like to write 'love me' across our T-shirts. Everyone likes to know that someone is very interested in them. We all like to be special to someone, someone we have chosen. We need closeness, a relationship of sharing, of trust. For most of us, in the end, the relationship where we will experience that most completely is in marriage. But that might be a long way off yet.

Meanwhile, in our society 'going out' bridges the gap. It's more than friendship, it's not yet marriage. It might or might not lead to marriage.

A Christian has to ask himself or herself some questions about going out with a particular girl or boy, and about 'going out' in general. Jesus turns a lot of ideas upside down. He teaches, 'You have heard it said . . . but I say . . . '. This is going to be true about 'going out'. He always has a better way, a way in which you will be more free to be your real and best self. So it is exciting to look for it. Like making a sculpture out of marble, finding the way will be very hard work but will be worth it. The result will be beautiful.

The fact is, a special relationship with a friend of the opposite sex can help or harm. It can be good or bad in the long run. The snag is, you might not realize at the beginning of the relationship which it is going to be. That's why you need your wits about you. That's why you need to know – beforehand, preferably – the patterns Jesus has laid down for your good. *How* you 'go out' or don't 'go out' can also have a very big influence on your whole Christian life, making you either stronger or weaker. What you do now will affect your life later. Here are some of the questions you might ask yourself.

Am I *depending* on going out with somebody in order to feel I am valuable, or nice, or attractive?

Your relationship will be better if you accept the value that God's love has already given you. Then you will not be desperate to have someone else prove what you are worth. You will already know it. You needn't be totally amazed to find that someone likes you. You needn't be *completely* devastated if the person you like doesn't seem to have a special interest in you.

Once you have really realized that you do not need to be going out with someone in order to prove your worth, you won't be so desperate to have a close relationship that you will go out with anybody! You won't mind waiting sometimes. You might even *prefer* not to go out with someone for a while. You will be able to continue your friendships and think carefully about whether to develop a particular one. You will also find that you won't be very happy with the kind of relationship that starts fast and has no foundation of friendship. You will want to build up slowly. 'Love' is meant to be a deep word, not a shallow one.

How can I know whether or not a particular relationship would be good to develop?

Placards don't normally come down from the sky with YES or NO written on them as you are prayng about it! But you do need to pray about your relationships – and not just after you have leapt in with both feet! It is sometimes very hard to hear what God wants you to know, especially when your heart is beating fast and loud! But God will make sure you understand what he is saying if you really want to hear him. As you get to know someone, you will see whether the relationship could develop and be good. If your ears are open to God's voice you will be careful not to develop a relationship which you know deep down would not be helpful.

It is important, too, not to give the other person the wrong impression. You can easily give someone the impression – by how you look at them, speak to them and treat them – that you want to 'go out' with them. Don't give that impression, until you know it's true. This is not being unnatural, it's actually being more natural, more honest. It might be hard, because lots of people around you are saying more than they mean by their attitudes, words and actions.

What am I 'going out' with someone for?

Sorry if that sounds an obvious question. We've partly answered it by saying that people like to be special to someone. Is that your only reason for going out with someone, or do you really value their friendship? It's good to get to know someone really well. If you learn good friendships now, you will experience good relationships later. I'm emphasizing the friendship aspect of a relationship again, because I think it's the most important.

When you go out with someone, you can be interested in their interests and they can be interested in yours. That way, you might double your interests! He might know a lot about music, and you may become fascinated with it. She might be heavily into drama, and you may find yourself drawn in. One of you might like cycling, and encourage the other to have a go. The other might be an ace at table tennis, and you don't mind being beaten for the tenth time. With a friend, you are more likely to get round to doing something, or going somewhere, you've had in mind for a while. You can also be interested in each other's friends, and so double the number of your own! Going out with someone will have a big effect on you – for good or bad, or both. A relationship which is formed for the wrong reasons can harm your character: it can damage your emotions, undermine your confidence, leave you feeling insecure and make it difficult to trust someone again. It can cause you problems later on in marriage. It can weaken your spiritual life. Relationships like this should carry a government health warning!

A relationship that develops from a basis of friendship can be wholesome and encouraging. It can help your emotional development, create a sense of self-worth and respect for people of the other sex. It can help you to learn to relate to someone in a way which would blossom later on in marriage.

The next few chapters will help you concentrate on the helpful kind of relationship, and avoid the harmful kind.

## Talking point

Think of some people you know who are 'going out'.
What do you think their reasons might be?

# 8
# Your relationship and other people

The person who has been deeply aware of his sin and his unworthiness of God's love, knows how valuable he is in God's sight. Jesus has died for him; he is of enormous worth. This person sees other people in a new light. He sees their infinite value and importance. A Christian should never want to trample anyone down – in thought, word or action. He should never treat another person lightly or as less significant than himself.

Were you ever the kind of child who had one little friend and wanted to keep that friend all to yourself? Were you jealous if that friend paid too much attention to anyone else? There is a danger that such a person can become far too possessive later on with a girlfriend or boyfriend. If you weren't that kind of child, don't start to be like it now!

We live in a society which encourages this kind of attitude. We are led to think that the greatest goal in life is an 'ideal' relationship with someone of the opposite sex. According to this view, boy–girl love is more important than anything. Other relationships matter very little in comparison. It gives you the right to let your friends down, to deceive your parents and even to compromise your moral standards in favour of what seems now to be the ideal relationship. Of course, this kind of attitude contradicts what we have said about the importance of people. But have Christians taken up this attitude to some extent? Do you sometimes let friends down because you would rather be with your girlfriend/boyfriend? Have you almost abandoned a friend for a time because you were swept off your feet by someone else and thought that was more important?

A totally exclusive relationship like that is off to a bad start. It becomes boring in time! No one person can supply you with enough interests, points of view and ideas to keep you going. If you doubt that, imagine being stranded on a desert island with her or him. A great idea, perhaps, to start off with, but think a year ahead, two years . . . You would run out of things to talk about! You both need the encouragement and stimulus of other people's company for your relationship to develop. So even from a purely selfish point of view, a friendship which completely cuts off other people will not be helpful to you. In many ways we learn about ourselves from other people, and different people develop and bring out good qualities in us. A good relationship develops and gets better because of the contributions of *others*. Exclusive relationships are usually very tense, and often full of rows. Often a heartbreaking separation is at the end. The rubber band, already stretched too far, snaps. A good relationship, on the other hand, can actually help you to get to know other people. If you are rather shy, you can feel more confident and able to make new friends when you have somebody beside you.

From everybody else's point of view, too, an exclusive relationship puts you on a bad footing. There is no greater pain in the neck than a couple who are so engrossed in one another's company that the rest of the world might as well not exist! Everyone wishes they would go somewhere else. And they might or might not be physically wrapped round each other. Mentally is bad enough! It is clearly wrong to neglect everyone else for the sake of that one person, however important that person might rightly be to you. When two people sit with their arms round each other, or one on the other's knee, or kissing, they are expressing their own personal relationship. This says to everyone else 'Go away, this is private, this is between us two.' (Unless of course it is just showing off.) Clearly that is not appropriate when the two are part of a group. People are not sure how to treat them; do they want to be included in the conversation or not? This can be very damaging to the group. It's interesting that many pop groups, when they are travelling from one place to another, do not allow girls in the van. This is because it spoils the group atmosphere to have a couple separating off and being wrapped up in each other.

'There is a time for everything and a season for every activity under heaven . . . a time to embrace and a time to refrain' (Ecclesiastes 3:1,5). We all need to learn what these times are. You can never say 'It's my own business' when you're a Christian.

We are not given the right, as Christians, to throw God's principles overboard, and give all our love to one

35

person. Love is a strange thing, though. The more we give away, the more we have left to give. So we can't lose!

To be practical, how do you go about making the best of other relationships when you are going out with somebody?

## Parents

'It is your Christian duty to obey your parents, for this is the right thing to do' (Ephesians 6:1, Good News Bible). 'Respect your father and your mother' (Exodus 20:12, GNB).

How do you make the best of your relationship with your parents when you are going out with someone?

The vast majority of parents want to meet him or her. They will feel happier if they know who it is you are out with. They want to share your friends a little. This can, of course, be quite trying, especially if Dad drags out the story of when you were two and managed to get the potty stuck on your head, or the day when you dragged Aunty Mabel's tablecloth off, bringing her best china with it. However, you may need to grit your teeth and take it gracefully! You may not realize it at the time, but you are building for relaxed relationships with them in the future. If your boy/girlfriend spends time with them, they are more likely to feel confident in your relationship with him/her. If you avoid bringing him/her home like the plague, they will, understandably, be suspicious, and think there is something to be worried about.

Another thing, if you fling your tea down your throat every day and rush out with hardly a backward glance, your parents are likely to become disgruntled and feel you are using the house as a hotel. Parents are people who matter. If you give them a chance to get to know your girlfriend or boyfriend, and an atmosphere of friendship and trust is created, it can help your own relationship tremendously. You will be able to relax in this area of your life.

## Friends

Don't plan all your activities just for the two of you. Include others. And not just other 'pairs' – this can make those without a boyfriend or girlfriend feel even more left out. Enjoy group activities. You have a responsibility to your youth group. Spend time with your other friends *without* your girlfriend or boyfriend. Make sure your other friends, and particularly your close friends, realize that they are important to you. Show that you want and need their company. You do need it, in fact, and there may well be a time when the shoe is on the other foot and *you* are the one who doesn't want to feel left out!

'Each of you should look not only to your own interests, but also to the interests of others' (Philippians 2:4).

## God

The Christian's number one relationship is with God – or it should be. Far from making other relationships seem less important, a right relationship to our Father in heaven helps us to value other people very highly. Our aim is to please God, and that is done by loving and obeying him.

It is worth spending time working out how we can best do that in the area of boy-girl relationships. How do we bring our thinking into line with his laws and principles? How do the clear guidelines in the Bible relate to our particular situation? They do. Don't be tricked into thinking that God has nothing to say on the subject; there are several principles which it is important to think about. For example:

'*This is love for God: to obey his commands*' (1 John 5:3). That includes, '*You shall have no other gods before me*' (Exodus 20:3).

Could a boyfriend/girlfriend be a god for you, in the sense that you would do what he or she wanted you to, even if you had a good idea it was not what God wanted you to? For example, '*Let us not give up the habit of meeting together, as some are in the habit of doing . . .*' (Hebrews 10:25). Would you go where he/she wanted you to, if it meant missing church, or some other fellowship group you owed your presence to?

'*Be concerned above everything else with the Kingdom of God and with what he requires of you . . .*' (Matthew 6:33, Good News Bible). Does your relationship with your boy/girlfriend tend to be a distraction from, or a substitute for, getting to know God better and therefore growing spiritually? Honestly?

You can work on it, if your girlfriend or boyfriend is willing to as well. If not, and if you want to develop as a Christian, there is nothing for it but to leave that situation. Hard words for some, but it makes sense in the long run.

On the other hand, your relationship may help you as you develop as a Christian. You may encourage one another to become more involved and active in church. You may even be able and willing to take on responsibility together to help with something.

As you learn to trust each other, you will be able to talk about spiritual things and share your thoughts openly and honestly. You can discuss what you have thought, read and heard this week. You can spur one another on. You can help one another to become more caring for other people. You can pray together, perhaps including others. You can talk to non-Christian friends about your faith, as they ask questions, and as the chance arises naturally. You can read the Bible together.

'Then those who feared the Lord talked with each other, and the Lord listened and heard' (Malachi 3:16). Keep an eye on yourselves. Is your spiritual life developing in this way? You may have to make a deliberate effort to use your relationship in a positive way. Some young Christians 'going out' together find it hard to talk to each other about the Lord they both love. If it doesn't come naturally, you will have to work at it. You can work together in God's kingdom, perhaps visiting and helping older people you know, perhaps encouraging each other to give away some of the money you might have spent on each other. See your best friendships – with either sex – as a way of helping each other grow as Christians.

---

## Talking point

What problems can arise in relationships with parents or friends when you are going out with someone? In what ways can you encourage your friends and/or your boyfriend/girlfriend in their relationship with God?

# 9
# Going out with non-Christians

Do you believe the Bible? I need to ask that at the beginning of this chapter, because if you don't, there is no point reading it. What follows is based on what God says in his Word, and some may find it hard to accept because it can be difficult to put into practice.

You may have already read or heard quoted, 'Do not be yoked together with unbelievers' (2 Corinthians 6:14). Whatever that *doesn't* apply to, it obviously applies to marriage. If marriage isn't a yoke, what is? A yoke is for holding two oxen together as they work, so that they go in the same direction and pull the plough in a straight line. If they didn't have this piece of wood holding them in place they would easily go in different directions and make a wonky line! So in marriage, a man and woman are linked together in such a way that if one goes in one direction, the other goes along too.

This is true literally: if one moves house, of course the other does too. It is also true in other ways: if one spends a lot of money on possessions, the other is drawn in. If one feels care for the elderly is important, the other is involved. And so on.

God knows that a Christian and a non-Christian don't 'fit together' comfortably, as if yoked. Without doubt, one will want to pull one way, the other another. The Christian has different reasons for the choices he or she makes. This doesn't only apply to obvious matters like a job, where to live, where church and prayer fit in. It also applies to the whole way you live, your attitude to other people, being a parent, using your money, eating your cornflakes . . .!

This is not the only passage in the Bible that makes it clear that God's people shouldn't marry outside the 'household of faith'. It runs through the Old Testament, and when God's people did marry those who did not share their faith there were a whole lot of problems. When they came to their senses they were really sorry, and realized they had done something very wrong (see Ezra 10).

Many non-Christians would understand this. They would think it obvious that if someone has an 'interest' or faith, which is so important to them that it takes up so much of their life, they wouldn't possibly be able to marry someone who didn't share it. Think about someone who was going to live on a houseboat. Could they marry someone who hated boats? If they did, either they would have to leave the boat or persuade the other person to live with them on the houseboat. Either way, it doesn't look like being very successful! It is actually more clear-cut than that with Christians and non-Christians.

What some Christians do is to marry a non-Christian

and hope that he or she will become a Christian eventually. This does occasionally happen. God is gracious, and sometimes does things which put right the wrong we have done. But that's no reason for deliberately doing wrong!

In Old Testament times different races of people worshipped different gods, so God's command was not to marry into those races. He knew that they would bring those other gods with them into the marriage. 'Do not intermarry with them. Do not give your daughters to their sons or take their daughters for your sons, for they will turn your sons away from following me to serve other gods . . .' (Deuteronomy 7:3,4). In the New Testament, Christians are instructed not to marry non-Christians for the same reason. They bring 'other gods' with them. It doesn't necessarily mean the other person is less nice, or not so good, or anything like that. It does mean your God is not their god. And the clear command is 'do not be yoked' with them. Or, as the Good News Bible puts it, 'Do not try to work together as equals with unbelievers, for it cannot be done. How can right and wrong be partners? How can light and darkness live together?' (2 Corinthians 6:14). There is no way round that, it is straightforward and clear.

But you aren't thinking of marriage at the moment – nothing is further from your mind. So is there anything wrong with going out with someone, just because they are not a Christian?

Some Christians say there is no need to get so steamed up about this because, after all, the kind of boy–girl relationship we are thinking of is little more than a friendship and has nothing to do with marriage. It isn't going to plunge you suddenly into all sorts of sin. The way some Christians behave when they are going out is much worse, these people say. Often Christians who say this are already going out with a non-Christian and are trying to defend their position. They may not have faced up to the real questions.

Another way of looking at it is that you can't share the deepest things, the things that matter most, with a non-Christian, and therefore the sort of relationship you would expect when two people are going out is not really possible with a non-Christian. It's important that you think this through carefully, before you leap to any conclusion.

The starting point has to be that it would be wrong to marry a non-Christian. Not only would it be unwise, it is clearly forbidden by God, who knows best. So then, of course it would be wrong to become engaged to a non-Christian because that is a promise to marry, which you can't make. But would it be all right just to go out with a non-Christian?

Let's look closely at what's involved before we try to answer that question. The nature of boy–girl relationships is that they develop. That's why they are so interesting. That's why it's so exciting having a good relationship. You are always learning new things about each other, always getting to know each other better.

Would you rather start off on a developing relationship with a Christian or a non-Christian? There seems to me to be only one conclusion. If you set off on a relationship with a non-Christian, it is going to develop. As it develops, the problems increase. The further involved you are, the harder it is to get out. There comes a point of no return. You may not be thinking of marriage now, but you can't be sure that the relationship you start now won't lead to marriage in three, four or five years' time. Or if not to marriage, to a 'yoke' in the sense that you will be tempted and pulled off course – in how you spend your time and money, how you

43

relate to other people and each other, for instance. The things which were the most important for you become less important. Your loyalties are divided.

If your relationship became serious, when would you break it off? When you are thinking of marriage? At that stage it would be very hard, almost impossible (though some have done it, at great pain to themselves and their partner, to avoid getting in a worse mess by marrying a non-Christian). That's one of the difficulties. The closer you are, the harder it is to separate.

That leads to a second difficulty. It is not fair on the non-Christian to carry on a relationship which you do not intend to develop into marriage, when that might be what he or she wants. It is playing with his or her feelings and life, as well as your own. You are acting as though you want to get more involved, when you know deep down you can't. The more you think about it, the more obvious the answer is.

What happens in practice? Sometimes a Christian goes out with a non-Christian and hopes he or she will become a Christian. The Christian is naturally very pleased when the other person shows an interest or comes to church, or seems generally sympathetic. So the Christian is optimistic enough to continue the relationship, in the hope that it will all work out. He or she gets more and more involved until there becomes no question of backing out. Very occasionally, the other person does become a Christian. Much more often, the Christian's position becomes weaker, and their faith ends up being just a hobby, a little part of their life, and then perhaps no part at all. This is one of the greatest tragedies. What the Christian has won is so little, compared with what he or she has lost.

Something else can happen: Jim and Sarah have been going out for two months. She is a keen Christian. It's all new to Jim, and because he likes and admires Sarah he thinks there may be something in it. They chat a bit about her faith. He comes along to church on Sunday evenings. As time goes on, he appears to be getting more interested, and to be asking important questions. He is coming to the youth group now and enjoying it, though he is a little bit on the fringe at times. Sarah is no less keen as a Christian than she has ever been. Tony is also a member of the youth group. He has just moved to their town. Sarah finds herself getting into interesting conversations with Tony.

They can have a good laugh together. She still brings Jim along, but finds she is spending more time with Tony. Eventually she realizes where this is leading, and tells Jim she doesn't want to go out with him any more. Shortly afterwards she is going out with Tony. Jim of course is hurt and upset. He wants to put it all behind him, and prefers not to see Sarah. He also finds that he feels angry with God, that somehow God and Sarah have both let him down. He certainly doesn't want to go to church, where he will see Sarah, and worse, Tony and Sarah. He has a strong reaction against the 'Christian stuff' he was becoming interested in. He will be much harder to reach now. In his mind, the emotional upset of his relationship with Sarah is all mixed up with his emotions about God. So that's that.

Because someone seems to be interested in Christianity, it doesn't mean they will become a Christian. Even if they become very interested and involved, they are not a Christian until they are born again. You don't know which way they will go. You should think carefully before encouraging a non-Christian to become emotionally involved with you. It could damage him or her as well as you.

Parties are often the way people link up in the dating

game. We've already seen some of the pitfalls of getting involved in such a superficial way, without getting to know each other first. And parties might hold a particular temptation for you to be like everyone else, to get drawn in and be compromised in a way you might regret. It depends on the sort of parties your friends go to. You might have to do some hard thinking on that. Can you go and not get drawn in? The answer might be different for different people, and for you at different ages. Know what you can cope with, and don't play with fire. For many, it's the way they started going out with a non-Christian. They didn't intend to, it just 'sort of happened'. In other words, they didn't feel strong enough in that situation to stand out and be different.

Get all this business about relating to non-Christians clear in your own mind. Don't put it off. The way to find out is not by doing – that could lead to disaster.

---

## Talking point

What is a yoke?

# 10
## How far do you go?

If your relationship has grown out of a friendship, you will have a lot in common with your boyfriend or girl-friend. There will be things to share, things to do together, places you would both like to go. In short, you will be busy! That is a good thing, and will help your relationship to grow.

You will also want to express something of how you feel about each other. It means a lot when he lends you his favourite record. You are pleased when she comes to watch you playing football. Practise ways like that of showing your feelings.

Have you ever played a game where the group playing have invented the rules? It might be your own version of beach cricket. As long as everyone agrees what the rules are, and accepts them, the game works. Some groups of young people have made up their own sets of rules for how you get involved physically in a boy-girl relationship. Most people seem to accept the rules – and in fact are afraid to play any other way. But what if the rules have been made up for the wrong reasons and are therefore wrong? If you are a Christian, you need to realize this is a possibility and work out what 'rules' would please God. Jesus turns many of the world's rules upside down, and nowhere more than in the area of relationships. His love never goes sour or wrong, so he can best point out where we could make mistakes.

The 'rules' that people make could vary considerably. They might say, for example, that you should kiss the first time you go out, move on from kissing as soon as you can, and only stop short of sexual intercourse. For some people, the rules would say you don't even stop there. **Don't blindly follow those rules. They might be wrong!**

It's important to know what's happening. All around you the standards of other people are affecting you, often without your realizing it. There are 'rules' being set, and you might be under strong pressure to conform to them. You don't have to! But you will need to be very clear in your own mind, if you are to resist the pressure.

Why do people kiss the first time they go out? Very often it's because they think they have to. It's the rules. Do you think it's good? The girl might feel pressurized by the boy, afraid that he will be less interested in her if she doesn't let him. The boy might feel pressurized by what his friends would think – he needs to show he's really one of them.

Think about these questions. How well do you know each other? Do you (really) want to express something in a kiss? Are you asking the other person to respond in a way she (or he) is not ready for? Do you care for each other, or is it the kiss you want, like diving into half a pound of your favourite chocolates?

Perhaps it's here that the problems can start. If you kiss too soon, and without a great deal of meaning, there is a real possibility you will become bored with that, and will want to go further. If you wait, and kiss only when you really mean it, that will be special and express something of what you really want to say about your feelings for the other person. Because it's for their sake and not its own sake, you will be better able to see the value of leaving it at that. In three words – **no cheap kisses**!

Looking back, it will be the gentle smile, the light touch, the quick hug which will have shown you he/she cares. Not the grabbed kiss, or anything you felt pushed into.

In Bible times they knew little of the long drawn-out stage between growing up and marriage – with rare exceptions, like Jacob waiting seven years to marry Rachel! (See Genesis 29.) Generally, it's something which goes with our society. You are, in a way, old enough to marry. But you have not yet been given adult responsibility. So you are not ready to take on the responsibility of a home and marriage. And you might want to do other things first, like finish your education, or get established in a job, or become an ace at a sport. You have grown up physically, but are not expected to marry until later. And in between, you need to know how to go about your boy-girl relationships. It's an odd custom, too, which encourages you to get close to one person, and then another, and possibly a string of people, before you actually decide on one, and marry her or him. We are in one sense trying to find out God's rules for a game he did not invent! But the principles in the Bible stand for all time. We only need discover how they apply to our own situation. It is certain they do apply. One thing is clear: 'going out' is not marriage. It may lead to marriage, or it may not. You are aware that either is possible. So you should not 'pretend' at marriage in any way. In marriage, two people become 'one flesh' (Gen 2:24). They then have responsibility for each other. They belong to each other. Before marriage you do not belong, though your relationship might be very special.

In particular, outside of marriage your bodies do not belong to each other. You shouldn't act as though they do. You have no right to ask of the other person something they don't want to give. And they have no right to ask of you something you feel you shouldn't allow.

In asking 'How far should we go?' sometimes young people are avoiding facing up to what is obvious. Sometimes what they mean is, 'I want to go further than I know I should. Can I?' Do think about your reasons for asking, if that is your question. Who are you thinking about, yourself or the other person?

Relationships are not like a yes/no questionnaire. They are not only about what we do, but why we do it (or don't!). If you don't understand the reasons, you'll never be happy to play God's way. Because sex is so much talked about, sung about, and acted on stage and TV, it is not surprising that it's on people's minds a lot. More than is natural. So there's a danger it becomes too important in our relationships, and too important too soon.

There is an enormous pressure on you to conform to other people's ideas of how to behave. In resisting, you might at times feel like King Canute standing at the edge of the sea, and telling it to go back! Sometimes you feel as though you might as well not bother! Where

50

you need to start resisting is at the level of your mind. More of that later.

If you are realistic about your relationship, you will not express physically more than it is ready for. You will not go further in that area than you have in getting to know each other in conversation, in going places and doing things together. I think if there were no extra pressures, it would be obvious what that meant. But because there are 'voices' telling us that we should be behaving in a particular way, it will help to spell out more clearly how we should show affection and love for a boyfriend or girlfriend.

Roughly speaking, there are two areas of physical expression. We'll call them 'affectionate' and 'strong' – for want of better words.

The strong area of expression normally belongs to marriage. Strong sexual feelings are aroused, which are meant to lead to sexual intercourse. Once you get into this area, you want to go further. The more involved you get, the harder it is to stop. That is what you'd expect. It's part of God's package for marriage. It's actually a bit of a cheat to go part of the way along this road, then stop. It's a bit like lighting a fire, then changing your mind and trying to put it out with an eggcupful of water. It's a bit like letting a tiger into your sitting room, then trying to put your hand over its mouth to stop it biting. Obviously you shouldn't have lit the fire or let the tiger in if you didn't want the consequences.

It is so important to think before you are in the situation. Decide before you lose your cool. Be clear in your own mind what is good. And stick to it.

These are some of the things this will mean in practice:

**1.** Avoid being with your boyfriend/girlfriend in situations you might have difficulty coping with. These could include babysitting together, or listening to some kinds of music. They might vary from one person to another. You need to know yourself – and your boyfriend or girlfriend!

**2.** Make *absolute* rules for yourselves, like:

- No lying down together.
- No form of petting, which is meant to lead you on further, and so strains the relationship.
- No undressing, or hands under each other's clothes.

You could add to the list, it isn't meant to be complete.

**3.** Be completely honest – don't kid yourself something is OK when you know it isn't.

**4.** Care about the other person. Don't lead them on so it is hard for them to stop. Everyone is different, and something you think you could cope with might be unfair on your boyfriend/girlfriend.

One young person told me, 'It's all quite obvious' meaning it's obvious what you should and shouldn't do. That's worth thinking about. We need to bear in mind the difference between knowing something is all right, and wishing it was all right. It is important that if ever we want to do something we are not convinced is right, we don't pretend to ourselves that we are not sure what is right or wrong.

You have, I think, an inbuilt sense of how involved you should get physically. It's not a very loud voice, though, and can be silenced. Listen to it. The best time to hear it is before you get into a situation where there may be choices to be made. When your emotions are shouting loud, you can't easily hear this other voice which might be saying, 'Just wait', 'Think about what would be better for him/her', 'Think about how you'll feel tomorrow', and similar things.

A relationship is only ready for close physical sharing when there is a deep commitment of every part of life to the other person – and that can only be to the person you marry.

Beware! Some Christians think they would never go too far, that they are somehow immune. That is a very dangerous view, because it means you aren't ready to resist temptation when it does come. Christians have the same emotions as non-Christians. They are as much sexual beings as anyone else. They need to be as careful as anybody else – more so, if they are tempted to think they are above temptation. No one is able to resist too much pressure. If you care about your boyfriend or girlfriend, you will not want to put him or her under that pressure. You will avoid the situations that might become difficult.

You lose nothing at all by being too cautious, but you could lose a lot by being carefree and uncautious. Conscience is not a foolproof guide. It may have been twisted. But if conscience says 'no' to anything, it is usually saying the right thing in this area. There are exceptions, but they are few.

Traditionally, it has often been the girl who 'puts the brakes on'. Both the boy and girl should be ready to if necessary, though it is better not to put the other person in a situation he or she would find difficult to handle. It should never be thought it is for the sake of the girl. It is for the sake of the relationship, and both people involved. The way sexual feelings are aroused varies from person to person. Some people (boys and girls) are easily aroused. Some girls are surprised how quickly some boys are turned on. They may be hurt by roughness, lack of gentleness, seeming to want something for themselves, even if the girl would prefer not to get that involved. It is the responsibility of both to avoid letting that happen. Each person should try to help the other. Some boys are surprised by how much some girls need to be reassured that they care. They need to understand that it isn't only physical involvement that will give them that reassurance. In fact it can give the message that it isn't really the girl they care about at all, but the excitement of the physical contact.

What if someone won't take 'no' for an answer? When you are the only one who wants to be restrained? Stick to your standards, and make them clear to the other person. You will not lose him or her – unless it was only your body they were interested in. He (or she) will respect you the more, and be glad afterwards.

It would be a pity to get so hung up about how you express your relationship physically that you didn't work on the other aspects of the relationship. Too much physical involvement too soon, stifles the rest of the relationship. Love gets left behind, and has increasing difficulty catching up.

The affectionate area of expressing your relationship is the appropriate one. You can be happy and relaxed together, sharing a hug or a kiss. This can be just right to say you care, you are very interested in the other person. You are glad you know them, they are special. You needn't become preoccupied with the way you express your affection. It comes naturally, because it is real. You don't need a list (it would be short anyway!). You are not saying, 'How far . . .?' That doesn't become an urgent question if you stay in the realm of affection. A relationship like this expresses warmly what it has to say, and can be full of meaning. It wants a natural and honest deepening of every aspect of the relationship, and does not let the physical side pull it out of shape or take over. If two people spend a lot of time together in complicated clinches, they need to stop and ask whether there is anything else to their relationship. Or is it just shallow, involving few shared interests?

Kissing is not a hobby, and shouldn't be treated as an evening's entertainment! It's not something you do, so much as something you want to say to the other person, and that they say to you. Otherwise it has little meaning or enjoyment.

Love and respect will bring you closer. An obsession with physical involvement and what might become lust, will only put barriers between you. Those barriers are lack of trust and respect, a fear of the other person. You should be able to trust each other in this area. It's not just a question of what you do or don't do. Everything you do has a deeper meaning, a reason. Learn the right attitudes, and you will want to do the right things.

'Every good tree bears good fruit, but a bad tree bears bad fruit. A good tree cannot bear bad fruit, and a bad tree cannot bear good fruit'(Matthew 7:17,18). If you haven't yet been out with anyone, you are in the happy position of being able to work out your ideas before you do. Be very clear in your own mind.

Be yourself – in the truest sense. Relax and don't think you have to behave in a certain way. Be determined never to let your friends or your boyfriend or girlfriend pressurize you into behaving in a way you are uncomfortable with. Go slow, in all parts of your relationship. Don't get too deeply involved too soon.

If you are going out with someone, or have had a girlfriend or boyfriend in the past, you might have got mixed up about some of the things we have said. You need to take a long hard look at what you did and why, and at your attitude to the relationships. Here are some important thoughts for you:

- It's not wrong to say no.
- Slow down, if you think you are getting too heavily involved.
- Talk to your boyfriend or girlfriend about it, and decide together on a better way.
- Be prepared to wait – you often have to, for something good.
- Remember that part of the fruit of the Spirit is self-control (Galatians 5:23). Ask for it in prayer – and be willing to receive it!

This is the area of life where many young Christians have problems, and where some are least willing for God to be in charge. It's often a testing-ground. *Are you willing to hand this very important area of your life to him*? If so, it's likely you will also give him the less important ones. Most people have strong feelings about the opposite sex, maybe one of them in particular! If you will allow those feelings to be under God's control, it shows you want him to rule in your whole life.

Here is some of the bad advice you may get from your friends, the big screen, certain music. Some answers are also suggested to start you thinking:

**1.** If you love him or her, do what you both like.
*Answer*: If you really love him or her, you will want to do what will be for his or her good and yours, in the long run, and not just react to how you feel today.
**2.** You need to be natural, to let your feelings run in any direction they like.
*Answer*: Sometimes we are 'naturally' wrong!

**3.** You must express yourself. If you feel a certain way, show it!

*Answer*: You need to control your sexual feelings so they can develop at the right time and in the right way.

**4.** Your sexual behaviour should never make you feel guilty. It's prudes who have surrounded sex with guilt.

*Answer*: It's very true that some people, especially in the past, have made people feel that sex is nasty. God doesn't say that – he made us as sexual beings. He says it's good, and you should only feel guilty if you use it wrongly. But if you do abuse your sexuality, you should feel guilty.

God is holy, and he wants us to be holy: '. . . for it is written, "Be holy, because I am holy" ' (1 Peter 1:16). Being holy means being different, in ways we should be different. 'Your body is a temple of the Holy Spirit, who is in you, whom you have received from God' (1 Corinthians 6:19). You should 'honour God with your body' (verse 20). That means you shouldn't do anything with your body you wouldn't like God to know about (he does know, of course). It also means you are bringing dishonour to God's Holy Spirit when you commit sexual sin. You can't separate off that part of your life and say it has nothing to do with God, because his Spirit is in you. So show proper respect for him and what he wants, how he wants you to behave. Accept the leadership of God in that part of your life.

Your actions come from your mind. They also come from your will. If you want to please God in the sexual area of your life, really want to, he will help you. If you know what you want, and it's not God's will, the battle is already lost. If you're not sure, you need to become sure. It's at that level you need to sort yourself out.

We're all weak and could do wrong, if we were

tempted enough. So there are times when we have to run! Joe did just that, when his boss's wife tried to get him to go to bed with her. She asked him day after day, but he resisted and avoided being with her. He wanted to do what was right. One day when no one was around, she grabbed him by his clothes and asked him again. He ran off, leaving part of his clothes in her hand! (For the full story, see Genesis 39.) He knew that to run was the only answer. To stay where he might be tempted would have been foolish. Some of us are not so sensible. We might think we are stronger than we are. We don't disappear at the first sign of temptation. We play with temptation, perhaps because we have not decided what we really want to do. We then either give in to temptation, or have a much more difficult situation to get out of. There are times when we need to say, 'Let's go for a walk', or 'Let's go and see Sue.'

'Flee the evil desires of youth' (2 Timothy 2:22). Don't put temptation in each other's way. Don't deliberately arouse the other person's strong sexual feelings by:

- how you dress
- what you say
- what you do.

'Do not arouse or awaken love until it so desires' (Song of Songs 3:5). It would be wrong to go too far, and it would be a pity, for both of you. Be aware, for example, that a boy might be aroused by what he sees, more so than a girl, and a girl by touch.

God knows our weak nature and provides for it: 'So, if you think you are standing firm, be careful that you don't fall! No temptation has seized you except what is common to man. And God is faithful; he will not let you be tempted beyond what you can bear. But when you are tempted, he will also provide a way out so that you can stand up under it' (1 Corinthians 10:12–13). *He* doesn't put you in a situation where the temptation would be too much, so make sure you don't put *yourself* in a situation like that.

If you and your boyfriend find ways of showing that you care about the other person, you will feel secure with each other. There needn't be the pressure or the rush to get involved physically. You'll be happy to leave the 'strong' area for the person you marry.

If you were going for a special meal at a restaurant in an hour's time, it would be stupid to have a McDonald's and big chips and hot apple pie now. The meal would be rather spoilt for you! Don't spoil God's wedding present, sex, by trying to open it before the wedding.

---

## Talking point

The best thing you can do about this chapter is pray. It might be helpful to talk about it with your youth group, if you have one. Listen particularly to what people of the other sex, in the group, have to say.

# 11
# When it's too late

I'm including this chapter because some people reading this book might feel guilty. They might have gone wrong, in a big way or in any way they know is wrong. You might be thinking. 'All that makes sense, but it's too late.' You may feel you have gone wrong in the sexual area already, and made a mess. If that is so, the biggest lie you could believe is that because you have already done wrong, it doesn't matter what you do now. It matters as much as it ever did!

The first thing you need to do is really face up to what is wrong. Don't try to explain it away or blame someone else. Tell God about it. Be sorry, and say so to God. Then you can know he has forgiven you: 'If we confess our sins, he is faithful and just and will forgive us our sins and purify us from all unrighteousness' (1 John 1:9). That means we can start again. There might be things we have to live with, because our sexual behaviour affects us deeply, and affects at least one other person very deeply. But we can start again. God does forgive, and we have to forgive ourselves too. This is not a kind of sin God can't forgive for some reason. In that way, it's the same as any sin. He can and does forgive those who are really sorry. And he encourages us to do better next time.

There are a few things to beware of if we have gone wrong:

**1.** It would be easy to go back down the path we have made, and do the same thing again.

**2.** It is easy to despise ourselves for what we have done, and think, 'I've made a mess once (or more). I'm so horrible, it won't make any difference if I do it again.'

**3.** Other people might make it hard for us to be any different.

**4.** Other people might not forgive us, although God does.

**5.** We might have to avoid a situation which was 'safe' for us before, but has become 'dangerous', because of the temptation we gave in to there.

**6.** There may be memories which are painful or pleasurable. If these trouble you, ask God to take them away, so that pictures of the past don't harm you now.

Some of these are hard to live with. But the most important thing is that we have put things right with God, and have fully accepted his forgiveness.

Then there might be something to put right, or explain, to someone else. That can be very hard. You might need to say that something you did, you now feel was wrong. It's important to be clear, or he/she might expect you to behave the same way again.

To continue doing wrong is the sad alternative to

putting things right with God. It makes you want to hide from God, and perhaps try to blame him for the situation. You will be miserable and knotted up inside – however things may look on the outside. In the end your conscience can become dull and unable to get through to you.

Hopefully the message has sunk in. If we have sinned and are sorry, God will forgive us. This doesn't then become a reason to sin again but rather spurs us on to do what pleases him. It's great that he can free us from the past and help us to live in a way that he is pleased with.

---

## Talking point

Is anything too bad for God to forgive?

# 12
# Sex and marriage

John went out with Clare. He loved her and decided
he wanted to spend the rest of his life with her. On his
visits, he would sleep in the same room as her. Then
he slept in the same bed. And then they had sexual
intercourse. They moved in together, and stayed
together for a while. Then John felt he might have made
a big mistake. They had a lot in common, but not that
much. He moved out again.

Where did he go wrong? I'd suggest a few places!

1. By sleeping in the same room as Clare he was
opening himself up to temptation.

2. He didn't test his desire to spend the rest of his
life with Clare – he was in too much hurry.

3. He was not willing to take the responsibility for
his own decisions.

Marriage was there from creation. It was a simple ceremony, but it was there as God's design for the man and woman. The intention was (and is) one man, one woman – for life. They became 'one flesh' (Gen 2:24) – that is, they have sexual intercourse. This is what makes marriage marriage. It is not, of course, the only part of a marriage relationship, but the part that belongs to that relationship alone. This is why sex outside of marriage is wrong. So, for example, 'Do you not know that he who unites himself with a prostitute is one with her in body? For it is said, "The two will become one flesh" ' (1 Corinthians 6:16). It is wrong to unite in body with anyone but your life-long partner. So God feels very strongly about divorce as well. 'I hate divorce,' (Malachi 2:16). His intention is that once a couple are one flesh, they stay together for life.

We are told to 'flee from sexual immorality' (1 Corinthians 6:18). Older versions use the word 'fornication' which means sexual intercourse outside of marriage, so that is the kind of sexual immorality it is talking about. Remember Joe running away from that.

I suppose John and Clare might have thought they were entering a kind of marriage, though what happened later showed they were mistaken. They missed at least three important facts about marriage:

**1.** It is public. Other cultures might have much simpler ceremonies than ours, but in all societies people recognize and give backing to the relationship. They often use presents to show it, which is nice!

**2.** It is a covenant, that is, a binding agreement between two people. Both take each other so seriously they want to promise themselves to the other for life. The congregation are the witnesses of that promise.

**3.** It takes on responsiblity for the other person. As

they become 'one in flesh' they take on the job of caring for the other person, whether they are ill or well, have difficulties, change their ideas, or disagree about things.

It is because sex is right and good as a part of marriage, that it is wrong in any other context. God is saying 'yes' to sex, which he invented, and putting it in the right place.

Marriage is where a man and woman are willing to come that close in their whole lives. They can have sex without fear and guilt, because they are committed to each other. It is not appropriate to express anything so intimate outside of marriage, because the other person might go away. There is not yet the trust and commitment needed for a life-long relationship, with its good times and bad times. You have not yet decided to share everything, always.

It is good that we are required to make a definite commitment, in public, to the other person in marriage. Left to our own devices, we might rush into something we might regret; we might think on the spur of the moment that 'getting hitched' to this person would be good, but then change our minds when we had longer to think about it. So while it might seem inconvenient and frustrating that we have to go through a whole lot of preparation and waiting before we can finally get together, it actually helps make it clear in our own minds that we want this to be our life-long partner, and that we are ready to share responsibility for someone else's life.

There isn't just one verse in the Bible that makes it clear that sex outside marriage is wrong; it is part of the whole teaching about sex and marriage in the Bible. Much of it is positive rather than negative: how good marriage is, how it was God's plan from the first man and woman, how a person is to be satisfied with his/her marriage partner, the praise of a good marriage relationship . . .

It is taken for granted in the Bible that marriage is the only pattern for male-female living together. That is God's invention. Any other pattern is human invention. It is clear that anyone who is 'behaving improperly' towards his fiancée should marry her. There is behaviour which is appropriate to those who are married only. As far back as Genesis, man had problems with obeying God's way in this, just as there were problems early on with murder. No sin is new. There are times in history when a society has particular problems with particular sins. Many feel that our society has a particular problem with accepting God's order of marriage. The number of broken relationships backs this up. The church, and particularly young people in the church, have something to demonstrate to the world here, by their pure relationships, and by preserving marriage, not as a deadly institution but as a safe place for bringing up children and a strength to the community.

---

## Talking point

What are some of the reasons why people do not accept marriage as a basis for their sexual relationships? What are some of the reasons you could give to explain why sex should wait for marriage?

# 13
## The mind

It matters what goes on in there, whether anyone can hear it or not. How is your mind?

'Do not conform any longer to the pattern of this world, but be transformed by the renewing of your mind' (Rom 12:2).

If our minds accept everything that comes their way, they will be rubbish tips! I quite like taking things along to our local rubbish tip because there are some fascinating items there. It's amazing what people throw out! In fact, it's all very dirty and the smell is horrible. Some of us have minds like that. They are collections of all sorts of rubbish, some of it foul, some fascinating. They are due for a clean-up, for some of the rubbish to be burned or crushed.

The mind becomes full of rubbish in a variety of ways. What we see and hear affects us more than we might expect. We record everything. Not that we remember it all, all of the time, but it is there. It is stored in the 'back' of our minds, until something happens to make us think of it again. Things we see and hear have a habit of coming back to us.

You don't have to look or listen far to take in wrong pictures or ideas about sex. The bigger the screen, the more powerful the picture. We don't easily forget these pictures. We may find we are using them to think in a wrong way about a relationship we have or would like to have, a way which would damage the other person and lower their value.

Words and ideas can start to mould our thinking. Not all at once, but gradually. Words with music are particularly powerful. We can take them in without thinking about the ideas or deciding whether they are helpful or not.

You can't stop seeing or hearing altogether, even if you wanted to, but you can do two things:

**1.** You can choose what you watch and listen to. You have the power to say 'yes' or 'no' to many of the words and pictures which come your way. Here are some simple devices: • switch off • change channel • look away • close the book • turn the page • change the subject • throw the record away!

Sometimes you need decisive action. Don't just let it all float over you through laziness. Choose positively. What is enjoyable, harmless and clean? If you think 'not much', you don't yet know what you are missing!

**2.** You can test what you see and hear. Don't just accept it because it's on the screen or in print. Is it true? Is it right? Is it twisted? Is it helpful?

Philippians 4:8 says: 'Whatever is right, whatever is pure, whatever is lovely, whatever is admirable . . .

think about such things.' Don't spend all your time tutting about what is bad and harmful. That can be unhelpful in itself. Look for good pictures, music and conversation .

Not everyone reacts the same way to the same things. You need to be aware of your own reactions. It's not just that you see a film with sexual immorality in it, and you want to do the same. You might not (though one girl told me 'You wish it was you'). It's more the effect of seeing and hearing so much that is sexually immoral; your standards can get worn away little by little and you start to think that all that matters is sex. Other important things get pushed to one side.

How do you control your mind?

It's a start to admit it needs controlling. It's a start to be aware that there are things already in your mind, which you wouldn't allow yourself to say, so they need cleaning out.

It helps to remind yourself that God knows what you are thinking, even if no one else does. He knows what sort of a person you really are inside, and isn't interested in a superficial 'wash and brush up' of the outside.

'Be transformed by the renewing of your mind.' What is important is to let go of the thoughts you like but which you know you shouldn't. Ask God to remove them. He recognizes a genuine request. He knows if you really mean it. That might not be the end of your struggle; the thoughts might come back, and you'll have to send them away again. But you will be glad to be free. Wrong sexual thoughts are a trap, not a pleasure, in the end.

If you start to control your mind at this level, you will be able to keep watch for new thoughts coming in. The sentry will be at the door saying, 'Are you really allowed in?' and will turn them away at the doorstep, before they have a chance to do any harm.

There's an old saying, 'You can't stop the birds landing on your head, but you can stop them making nests in your hair.' Get it? You can't always be in control of what you see or hear, or maybe think the first time. But you don't have to dwell on it. You don't have to chew it over in your mind, picture it again, say it over to yourself. Let it go. Make sure it does go.

## Temptation

Temptation works through the mind. The thing about temptation is that it's not obvious. Most of us would think we could resist it, if it was. It's subtle. Usually it comes little by little. A thought crosses your mind and flits out again. Gently it creeps back in. It is polite: it will only stay if you want it, and it won't be much trouble. On this second visit it is more familiar, it doesn't shock you so much. But it's willing to wait to find out whether it can stay. After a while you are not sure. You were sure, and you were going to ask it to go, but now it doesn't seem so clearly wrong. Once the thought is thoroughly at home, the action doesn't seem so remote. Before, it was something other people did, but not you. It still is probably. Or at least, perhaps you were being a bit hard on yourself? Now you are a little confused. You are not sure any more. It seemed so wrong, but it is quite attractive, and may not be so bad after all. You let it hover about, you don't rush into anything. But perhaps the only thing to do is try it. Just once. Only to find out. Oh yes, think about it later to really work it out. Bang!

That is how any temptation can work. Sexual temptation is no exception. That is why it is so important to work out what you believe is right and wrong before you get into a situation where you might be tempted.

There will be warning signals. You will feel uneasy about what you are thinking. Your conscience will tell you something is going wrong. But it's up to you whether you take any notice or not. If you ignore the signals often enough, you won't hear them at all in the end.

Jesus summed it up: 'From within, out of men's hearts, come evil thoughts, sexual immorality, theft, murder, adultery, greed . . . All these evils come from inside . . .' (Mark 7:21-23). The message is that the inside needs putting right first, and the outside will automatically follow.

Thoughts lead to words. Thoughts lead to actions. Pure thoughts lead to good words and actions. Wrong thoughts lead to harmful words and actions. Don't allow patterns of thought to become ingrained: from there they are translated into actions, and actions become habits which are very hard to change.

'Do not give the devil a foothold' (Ephesians 4:27). You know what happens when a pushy salesman manages to get you interested in his product. He gets a foot in the door, and you are going to find it very hard to resist buying something. It's the first foothold that counts. If you give temptation just a little foothold the door is kept open, and you will find it hard to close it again.

You need to know your weak points. And take special measures to protect them.

---

## Talking point

Is there any temptation you would find it very hard to resist? What can you do to help yourself resist it?

# 14
# Learning to Love

Love is not something you fall into; it has to be learned. Most of us aren't very good at it, naturally speaking. We all like to be loved, that doesn't need learning. But giving love is another matter.

Somebody once said to me, 'I've been married fifteen years, and I'm only just learning what love is.' So you may have a long time to go! But you can start learning early on.

God has told us plenty about love. He has shown us plenty. 'We love because he first loved us' (1 John 4:19).

He has told us to love; it proves our love for him: 'For anyone who does not love his brother, whom he has seen, cannot love God, whom he has not seen' (1 John 4:20).

A lot of what makes up male-female love is the same as any other love. It should not be thought of as something completely different, or you will miss some of the main ingredients. Here are some of them: 'Love is patient, love is kind. It does not envy, it does not boast, it is not proud. It is not rude, it is not self-seeking, it is not easily angered, it keeps no record of wrongs. Love does not delight in evil but rejoices with the truth. It always protects, always trusts, always hopes, always perseveres' (1 Corinthians 13:4-7).

We'll take a look at some of these ingredients, and how they apply. If we could master them we could be good lovers. It's interesting to notice that lust is completely the opposite. Lust is impatient, lust is unkind. It is jealous, it is boastful, it is proud. It is rude, it is self-seeking, it easily gets angry, it keeps a score of wrongs. Lust delights in evil.

How did you score? Are your relationships built on love? No one has got it all right, not after fifteen or even forty years!

Let's take a closer look.

'**Love is patient**'. Perhaps the outing you planned together has to be called off, because a family event has been arranged for the same day. Perhaps you feel you want to spend all your spare time together, but know it's important to see other friends. Perhaps your boyfriend or girlfriend doesn't see the relationship quite as you do. Love is patient.

'**Love is kind**'. When the other person is tired, you take the load. When he is upset, you try to react in the most helpful way. When she is feeling inadequate, you encourage her.

'**It does not envy**'. Love actually encourages the other person to have other friendships, and is interested in them. Love is glad of the qualities of the other person, and helps them develop.

'**It does not boast**'. The last thing you will talk about to others are your exploits in love. And a person who loves would not try to say that he or she is better than the one who is loved.

'**It is not proud**'. It is willing to be in the wrong. It is not delighted that the other person might be wrong. It does not take all the credit. It is happy to expose something of its own feelings, and fears, and weaknesses.

'**It is not rude**'. Love does not barge into the other person's life at a rate they are unhappy about. It always takes account of the other person's feelings.

'**It is not self-seeking**'. Can you learn this? It is so hard. Love does not put *me* at the centre of the universe. It finds out what would be good for the other person, what would help him or her, and goes for that gladly.

'**It is not easily angered**'. Just because it can't have its own way, it doesn't go off in a huff. When the other person is less than perfect, it doesn't make a huge fuss about it.

'**It keeps no record of wrongs**'. It doesn't say, 'You always do that!' or 'You never come with me to see Steve!' because it has forgotten past wrongs. It concentrates on the present, and on better things to come.

'**Love does not delight in evil but rejoices in the truth**'. It takes no pleasure in doing wrong or in finding out the other person was wrong. It concentrates on what is true and good.

'**It always protects**' – the other person from harm, from influences which would hinder his or her growth as a Christian.

'**Always trusts**' – it doesn't act like a bodyguard to the other person. It encourages him or her in other activities. It believes the best of the person and expects the best.

'**Always hopes**' – has good expectations. Believes in

what the other person is and can do.

**'Always perseveres'**. Love knows it won't always have an easy time. It doesn't give up at the first sign of difficulty or disappointment in the relationship. It works at it, always.

Love is so positive. Think what it is like to be loved in all those ways, how it helps you as a person. You too can be used by God, who *is* love, for the great good of other people, and of the boy or girl who becomes someone special for you.

A close man-woman relationship is built on friendship. It is not a stage you can miss out. It will be the main ingredient of a good marriage. This love has to be learnt.

There is an idea about that love is something you get. If only we had love, if only he/she loved us. 'I love you' might only mean, 'Will you love me?' if we are not careful. Love is actually something you give, not something you get. (Though if you give love, you will get it.)

It is only fair to stress this side of love. The getting side is stressed enough. One girl told me she was marrying for the second time, and moving away. 'But if I don't like it, I can always get out.' We need an understanding of love which does not just concentrate on 'me', and how things will suit 'me'. To give love is a happy experience, as well as hard at times.

Some of the 'giving' qualities of love are commitment, responsibility, trust, respect, faithfulness, honesty. Think about each of these, and how far you have learnt them in your friendships. 'Each of you should look not only to your own interests, but also to the interests of others (Philippians 2:4). If it seems hard to learn that, it's also an adventure. You actually feel better if you learn to give, than if you only want to get.

You can 'practise' this kind of giving-love now. Don't wait for one ideal person to come along to give all your love to. You would have none left to give! Practise sharing what you think is yours with your friends. Practise surprising someone with a small present, a thoughtful act. When a friend of mine is buying some sweets for himself, he buys some for a friend or friends too. That guards him against selfishness and pleases someone else.

Giving love makes you lovable. If you become the kind of person who loves others, you will find that others love you.

## Talking point

What do commitment, responsibility, trust, respect, faithfulness and honesty each mean in a relationship?

# 15
# Afraid to Love

You are going to have to come out of there if you want
to love anybody! Are you in a shell, where you hope
other people will come and love you? There's no room
for two in most shells! You are going to have to do the
difficult thing and come out, if you want to make good
relationships, that is.

How do you come out? You stop thinking about yourself so much. You start thinking more about other
people. You don't worry so much about your appearance, your personality, even your comfort and your
needs. You let drop the worry about how other people
react to what you say and do. You stop minding so
much if you are misunderstood, or laughed at. You are
busy making friends. You might also be busy making
one friend in particular. You go out to them in the offer
of friendship. That doesn't mean you smother them

with your attention, or you chase them so they have no time and space to themselves. That is something different. But you ask them who they are, and are interested to find out. You want to know about them; they are interesting.

Shy people are sometimes the best listeners, and that can be very attractive. Not everyone wants to relate to the 'life and soul of the party' types. But everyone likes to know someone is listening to them. That is often more important than being able to come up with interesting conversation yourself. So practise listening if you are shy – or even if you are not!

If you have been hurt before, it's hard to love. Love is a risk: you let something of your real self show. If love develops at the right pace, not too fast, it is less painful, because little by little you find out a bit more about each other. As you do so you learn to trust each other, and you dare to say a little more, let a little more of your personality show, gradually and gently. Once you have shown a lot of the real you, you could be hurt. That is always the risk and that is why it's not a good idea to get too involved too soon. You will suffer hurts you needn't have. In any case, there will be pain in your relationship, there always is but it's often just 'growing pains'. Love grows painfully and joyfully at the same time. If you want the joy without the pain, it's not real love you are after.

Pain comes because two less than perfect people are coming closer together. They will bump into each other and move away. They will find they don't 'fit' with the other person in every single way. Someone will have to give way in every conflict. It's best if both give way a little. But it costs, even then.

Pain comes when that relationship is coming to terms with other important ones. The needs of parents and other friends might call you away from that relationship for a time. That could hurt. Sometimes in discussion you could side with someone else, and not the one you are learning to love. A mature love can cope with that, if it is done gently. A childish love doesn't feel sure enough of the other person to allow it.

Pain comes when the other person lets you down. He or she might not realize what they have done, but it still hurts. You learn what is painful for the other person, and will always be learning. Meanwhile it really can hurt.

'I have no need of friendship, friendship causes pain . . . If I never loved, I never would have cried' (Paul Simon, *I am a rock*). That is a choice you could make. But it's not God's choice for you, whether you wish to be single or married. God *is* love.

Don't let the risk and the pain come as a surprise to you. It's good to accept them early on as a part of every aspect of life, this side of heaven. But they are worth it for good relationships. And that is what life is all about in the end: relationships with people, and a relationship with God.

Boys in particular need to learn real friendships. Often, because of what people might think, boys shy away from friendship. They know what it is to play football with others, but they have not always learnt to share something of themselves. They need to take the risk and come out of their shell.

---

## Talking point

Which is harder, to stay in a shell, or come out of it?

# 16
# Boy-girl relationships - a god?

'Those who cling to worthless idols forfeit the grace that could be theirs' (Jonah 2:8).

What is an idol? Anything that takes the place that should be God's. An idol can be a thing, a person, an idea, a belief, a game . . . or anything else. The thing, whatever it is, may not be wrong in itself. It may be very good.

Gold is created by God, and good. To make an image out of gold and worship it is wrong. Today's idols are more subtle than that. We would not dream of worshipping something made of gold. But we might be tempted to put other things in the place that should be God's. If you watch TV constantly, when you should be doing something else, it becomes an idol. God wants us to worship him only.

It would be easy to feel we love someone so much

we would do what the person wanted, even if it contradicted what God had said. This is to 'idolize' the other person.

Some people make an idol, not of a particular boy-girl relationship, but of boy-girl relationships in general. They think of hardly anything else. They talk about them, read all the glossy mags, think and dream about them, spend all their lives thinking up tactics for catching the next girl or boy. The media (TV, radio, advertising, magazines etc.) encourage it. A car can't be advertised on the basis of its qualities, but by the girl draped seductively across the bonnet. What is wrong is not that it is a girl, but that she is there simply to distract. A link is made in your mind: 'nice' girl, 'nice' car. You don't actually buy the girl, just the car, but you are drawn to the car by the girl. The way some groups of young people talk about sex, you would think that was the only thing there was.

If you are surrounded by people who idolize that particular kind of relationship, you will need to be careful not to be drawn in. They may make you feel peculiar if you have not got a boyfriend/girlfriend. They may bombard you with talk about sex, or members of the opposite sex – seeing them not as people, but as sex objects. Or they may take a more romantic view of the other sex. But it seems to be the one topic of conversation. Your thoughts could become dominated in the same way.

Why do people 'cling' to idols? Perhaps because they have nothing else. They are looking for satisfaction, and hang on for dear life to anything which may seem to offer it. The writer of Ecclesiastes tried all sorts of things to find satisfaction – study, pleasure, 'great projects', silver and gold, sex – and found them 'meaningless, a chasing after the wind' (Ecclesiastes 2:17). They were not a means of satisfaction in life. The reason was 'because I must leave them to the one who comes after me'. Whatever good things life brings (and there may be lots), they are only enjoyed for life. There is something beyond that.

God has 'set eternity in the hearts of men' (3:11). Whatever we have, we have a longing for something beyond it. The most fulfilling and happy relationship leaves a desire for something more – and even points us towards someone more, who is God. We can only be satisfied with him. 'Those who cling to worthless idols' do so desperately, in spite of the fact that they know deep down there is more to life than that. It's a sad picture. Idols don't satisfy. Sometimes they seem to for a while, but it always wears off. A Christian is satisfied with a growing relationship with God. This should show itself in his/her attitude to boy/girl relationships. We all need other people. Christians are attracted to the opposite sex, just as other people are. Most will form a special relationship and marry. These things are good, and are invented and blessed by God. A Christian need not cling desperately to the idol of a boy/girl relationship, because it is not the only thing in life.

People who do cling to idols of any kind 'forfeit the grace that could be theirs'. It's not only that idols don't satisfy, but they make you miss out on other things God has in store for you. This is particularly true in the area of relationships. If you start a relationship which is selfish, you won't ever know what God might have wanted for you. There may have been ways he wanted you to serve him, with all the joy that could have brought. Or people you would have met, perhaps even a better relationship you could have spent your time on. If you disobey God in your relationships, you will lose out.

To keep boy-girl relationships in their proper place is a relief. It takes the pressure off: you don't have to try to pretend to be anything you are not. It stops you being narrow and from having a one-track mind. Instead, all kinds of other aspects of life are attractive and exciting, too.

A good relationship is not one which you cling to desperately. That makes for a very tense and untrusting relationship. A Christian's confidence is to be in God. A Christian's goal is the kingdom of God. As you make that the focus of your life, he gives you back all kinds of good things, including good relationships.

'Seek first his kingdom and his righteousness, and all these things (ie, the things you need) will be given to you as well' (Matthew 6:33). There is a dimension in a relationship between two Christians which is unique. Each one knows God, and God becomes part of the life of the pair together. They don't look to each other for the answer to life. Together they share Jesus, who is the answer.

---

## Talking point

At what point do boy-girl relationships become a god?

# 17
# The group experience - a dream?

Right at the start of this book I made it clear that 'going out' isn't the only pattern of behaviour in the world. There are countries where it simply doesn't happen. But it's probably the one which has surrounded you from your birth so you have grown used to it.

I worked with a Christian youth group for a while where none of the members were going out with each other. It was a small group, and they were all good friends. They could openly share their problems, hopes and ideas. They used to go out together for walks, to the ice rink, to the pictures, to someone's home. They had fun. They were happy. They loved each other. If one was upset, they were all upset. If one was excited about something, they could all share it. They were all different personalities, some quiet, some noisy, some creative, some brainy. They learned from one another.

Because they were all good friends they didn't feel under pressure to go out with someone just for the sake of it. That's what they said; that's how they felt. It didn't last for ever and eventually they went different ways. As they got older some left the town. But they had something special. They had learned to relate to people of the other sex at a deep level, without being too intense.

Is this something that works in your youth group (if you have one), or is it something that could never work? Could you help it to happen? Consider some of these ideas:

1. Invite the group round to your house or to someone else's, where everyone feels relaxed. Have some fun.

2. Suggest outings together – to a burger bar, for a walk, to the pictures . . .

3. Don't give up. If some people seem a bit apathetic they may need time to realize how much they could enjoy themselves. They may need time to get to know each other well enough to relax completely.

4. Pray about the members of the group. Are there some who feel a bit out of things, some who try to dominate it?

5. Above all, be positive. Don't just get together to moan about having nothing to do, or to bewail the fact that you haven't got a boyfriend/girlfriend. Use your imagination to think what you could do. Plan something definite, at least for the first few times.

There are things you don't know about the people you know. In a group you have the chance to find out more about them.

If there is someone in the group you are particularly keen on, get to know him or her as part of the group.

Invite her/him along with the others. That way your friendship can develop naturally without putting a strain on it. It is one of a number of friendships and may become a special one in time. Give it time.

It's not that you won't have any difficulties if you explore the group alternative. There will be times when you could scream. There may be times when you do scream! But it's worth working at it.

Within the group you'll find some people, of both sexes, with whom you get on particularly well. And so will everyone else. But no one is left out, because you are all part of the group. You work at getting on with everybody, because they all belong. Everybody is important.

A group like this can cope with one or two people in it who have particular needs. They may seem a little odd for all sorts of reasons. You might not feel able to spend a lot of time with these people on your own, but as a part of the group they are accepted and loved and can develop, and perhaps become less odd! And you too feel accepted and loved. People start to look forward to being with the group, not only because of particular people in it, but because the group is a good place to be. It's a laugh. It's somewhere you and the others can be yourselves.

If you haven't had this experience of belonging to a good group, give it a try. Allow time for it to develop into something worthwhile. The friendships formed in that way may last a lifetime, even though the group itself will eventually split up as people go their different ways. The group can go a long way to providing the relationships you need. It provides a social life. It gives a good setting for friendships to grow. It makes exclusive boy-girl relationships seem less important. Particular relationships will develop when they are ready, they don't need to spring up before time.

# Talking point

How could you go about getting your group to grow closer?

# 18
# Be different - be yourself

Are you 'caged'? Do you feel trapped into behaving a certain way? Perhaps you don't; perhaps you are trapped and you haven't noticed. If you are trapped, and are not being the kind of person you really want to be under God, you need to 'get free'.

Don't just conform to the behaviour you see around you. Don't fall into line with the morals some people would like to push you into. Do think for yourself. Be creative in your life. Feel free to be yourself, even if that is different from the next person. Be your good self, of course, not your bad self! Study God's ways and his framework for living, and make friendships which are full of the qualities of love in 1 Corinthians 13.

Dare to influence others for good. Many people are unhappy in their relationships partly because they can't trust each other and they can't trust themselves. Many young people simply don't know how to behave with the opposite sex, so they do what they see others doing. It makes them uneasy, but they have not found a better way. If they have some idea of what a better way would be, they haven't the courage to live like that. They are afraid of frightening off their boyfriend or girlfriend. They are afraid of what their friends might think or say. Some of them might join you very quickly if they saw you could relate to the opposite sex without using them. If they saw you being natural and yourself, they might be freed to do the same thing. Others might respond badly of course, and call you things you aren't. You might have to put up with that.

Both boys and girls often appreciate being able to talk about all sorts of things with someone of the opposite sex, with no strings attached. You might find yourself with friends you didn't know you had! Don't be wondering all the time what the other person is thinking about you. Be free enough not always to question where a particular relationship might lead. It's a case of enjoying it for where it is now.

Be really different – inside. 'Be transformed, by the renewing of your mind.' Change any wrong ideas you have taken in from what you have seen or heard, and think differently.

Then you will change outside, automatically. You'll be happier for it, and free (in a good, biblical sense). Your relationships will be deeper and richer. You are not being different so that everyone will notice you, you just want to be yourself. You might help others to be themselves too! It's great to know you are free to make your own decisions. Enjoy growing up and becoming responsible. Make it an adventure, not a bore.

Some churches are the worst places for gossip. They can turn your friendships sour without meaning to.

Some older people can't resist match-making. They don't give you the chance to develop relationships at your own pace. You have to be an individual to resist that, to insist on not being put off, on not being pushed into or away from a friendship.

'Don't let anyone look down on you because you are young, but set an example for the believers in speech, in life, in love, in faith and in purity' (1 Tim 4:12). Sometimes you have to be the one to show older people a better way. Surprise them by how you have thought out how you should live. Impress them (in the right way) by your commitment to your friends, and by the depth and maturity of your relationships.

Be different from the stifling patterns others or your feelings make for you. Be yourself in Jesus, free to care about others in a healthy and helpful way.

---

## Talking point

What are the pressures which might stop you being yourself?

# 19
## God's guidelines

This is a good time to put in a reminder of what God's guidelines are for male-female relationships.

God says **yes** to:
1. Marriage
2. Sex – within marriage
3. One man, one woman for life
4. Equal worth of the sexes
5. Love – lots of it
6. Friendship with both sexes
7. Appreciation of the other sex

He says **no** to:
1. Sex outside marriage
2. A lack of self-control in the physical aspect of your relationship – it abuses your own body and that of the other person.

**3.** A lack of self-control in *any* area of your relationship – it hurts you; it hurts the other person.

**4.** Exploiting another person

**5.** Homosexual acts

**6.** Getting 'yoked' with non-Christians, in any way

**7.** Lustful thoughts

---

## Talking point

Can you find some Bible passages which make it clear that these guidelines are God's?

# 20
## What about the future?

Sometimes thinking about the future is an escape from the present. However, it is helpful to consider how your life will develop without getting hung up about it. You need to put the future firmly in God's hands, where it belongs. '. . . You ought to say, "If it is the Lord's will, we will live and do this or that" ' (James 4:15).

Many young people haven't yet learned to do this. They have a dread of being alone in the future. That is natural. It isn't normal for us to live as isolated individuals. God never intended it that way. In our country we are not very good at relating to people around us, on the whole. Perhaps it is because of the cold climate – we stay indoors! So we may think of company only in terms of finding the right person to marry.

The Bible has some clear things to say about the pros and cons of being married. It also gives some of the reasons for both.

**Being single** means you can give more time to God's work. You can have a full and free commitment to what God wants you to do without having to consider what pleases a wife or husband (1 Corinthians 7:32-34). (In our culture of course many single people have other responsibilities to consider.)

One of the reasons Jesus gives for singleness is 'for the sake of the kingdom of heaven' (Matthew 19:12, RSV). Others may be widowed, or be physically incapable of a full married life because of injury or other handicap. If you are single you can enjoy a number of good friendships. You may be less restricted than the majority of married people and have opportunities for jobs, holidays and travel that you might not be able to attempt if you were married.

**If you are married** you are not alone. God designed male and female to be, in some ways, two halves of a whole. This is reflected in marriage. You have the sexual bond for pleasure and companionship. It is also for conceiving children, which are God's gift. If you are married, you have opportunities for working (and playing) together.

At a certain age you think all the advantages are on one side. Later you see that it is not like that; there are pros and cons for both. God says 'yes' to marriage, and 'yes' to singleness. Both are good gifts. 1 Corinthians 7:7 says: 'Each man has his own gift from God; one has this gift, another has that.'

Society says 'yes' to marriage or living together, but 'no' to true singleness. Sometimes even the church says 'no' to singleness, perhaps out loud, or perhaps in the way it treats people who are single. This can make some single people think there is something wrong with them, particularly in some countries. This is clearly against the teaching of the Bible.

You don't have to decide now whether you want to be single or married. It's quite likely that you haven't yet met the person you will marry, or found the direction God will lead you in the future, the work he has in store for you. Things unfold gradually, as a rule. One step leads to another. It's usually a mistake to take two steps at a time. If you met the person you were going to marry now, you might not even like her/him! God is working in you and in her/him. You will change and develop. When the time is ready, you will meet who you will meet. As Ecclesiastes 3:1 says, there is 'a time for everything . . .'

Your preparation for the future is to learn how to make good friends now – and how to be a good friend; to learn to love, and to grow in love, in God's way. If you make good relationships now the future will take care of itself. Or rather, God will look after it. And what you do now counts towards it. You can trust God. If you don't, you should learn to.

Above all, don't take short cuts because you think that God isn't hearing very well. When Abram became impatient with God because his wife Sarai hadn't had a child, he took the short cut and had a child by his servant Hagar instead. That brought a whole lot of problems later. His wife did have the promised child in the end. God knew what he was doing (Genesis, chapters 15-17, 21).

Waiting can be hard, very hard. Sometimes you know what you want, and you want it now! That can spoil the best thing that God has prepared for you in the future.

You may have to wait for a boyfriend or girlfriend. Don't go out with just anyone merely for the sake of it. You may be tempted to enter a strong sexual relation-

95

ship with someone. Put that temptation firmly to one side, and wait for the right time. You might have your own ideas about the ideal relationship and spend your time day-dreaming about it. Don't! You might miss the really ideal one which might creep up when you aren't looking!

If waiting is the hardest thing to put up with, it's also the most worthwhile in the end, because God will use it to prepare you for the best which he plans for your life.

Waiting might not be your problem, and that's great. You know that there are lots of important things to be getting on with and throwing yourself into – fun, friendship, God's work, study, hobbies . . . You are living life to the full and know that Jesus came 'that they may have life, and have it to the full' (John 10:10).

---

## Talking point

What do you think are the pros and cons of being single, and of being married?